D1545106

THE FACE OF PRAYER

THE FACE OF PRAYER

PHOTOGRAPHS BY

ABRAHAM MENASHE

ALFRED A. KNOPF   NEW YORK   1983

THIS IS A BORZOI BOOK PUBLISHED BY ALFRED A. KNOPF, INC.

Copyright © 1980, 1981, 1982 by Abraham Menashe

All rights reserved under International and Pan-American Copyright Conventions.
No part of this book may be reproduced in any form or by any means, electronic or mechanical,
including photocopying, without permission in writing from the publisher. All inquiries should be
addressed to Alfred A. Knopf, Inc., 201 East 50th Street, New York, N.Y. 10022.
Published in the United States by Alfred A. Knopf, Inc., New York, and simultaneously in Canada by
Random House of Canada Limited, Toronto. Distributed by Random House, Inc., New York.

Library of Congress Cataloging in Publication Data
Menashe, Abraham. The face of prayer.
1. Prayer—Pictorial works. I. Title.
BL560.M46 1983   291.4'3   82-48737
ISBN 0-394-52930-8
ISBN 0-394-71315-X (pbk.)

Manufactured in the United States of America
First Edition

INTRODUCTION

Prayer is a deeply personal act through which we commune, petition, reach out, and give thanks. This collection of photographs embraces the human family in moments of this intimate gesture.

Although prayer is present in all aspects of life, this book centers on the traditional religious form: a figure with clasped hands in the dark space of a church, pilgrims at the site of a shrine, a pious man dancing by a sanctuary. In each setting I have focused on the inward attitude rather than the outward rite.

The photographs were made in the United States, Mexico, Portugal, Israel, Singapore, and Bali. Each region contributed a view of humility; together they are bound by a common spirit, present when the human heart yields in reverence.

When we attend to prayer, its nature becomes known to us. We take refuge in stillness, and in our most naked state become receptive to a life force that nourishes, heals, and makes us whole again. To the extent that we have the courage to seek moments of solitude and listen to our inner voice, we will be guided by a light that lives in us. We come to know a love that does not disappoint—peace the world does not offer.

After taking a photograph in St. Patrick's Cathedral of a woman with tears in her eyes, I sat in the back and wrote, "Forgive me, Lord, for trespassing upon this moment. I've come here not to take but to share your peace."

Abraham Menashe

New York City, 1982

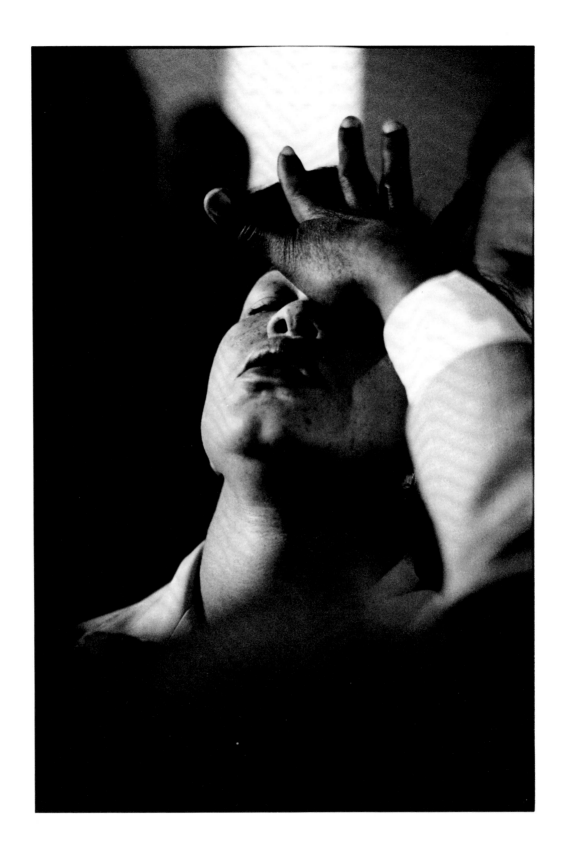

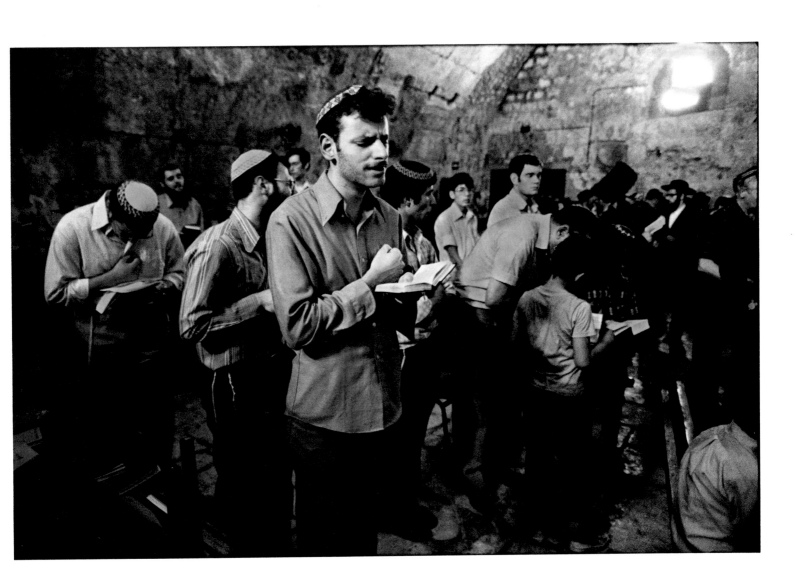

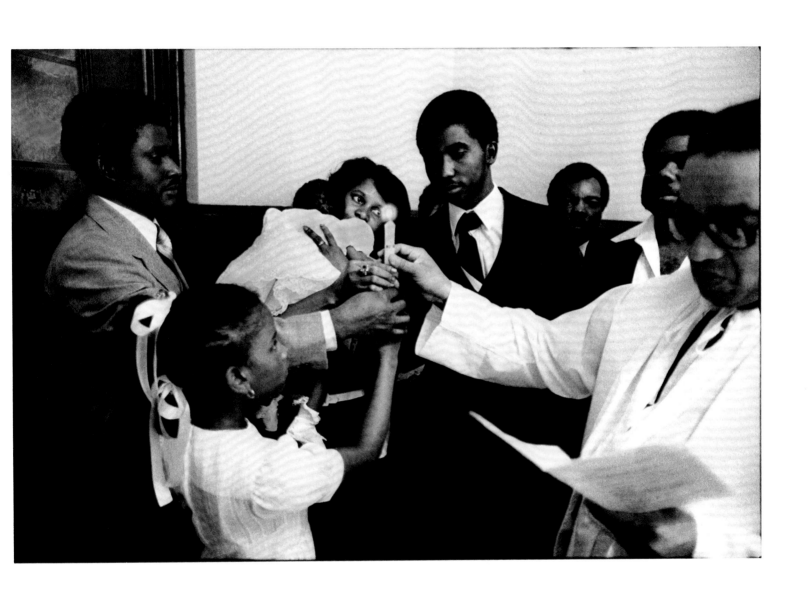

PICTURE SOURCES

ACKNOWLEDGMENTS

This book began when I was commissioned in May 1979 to create a photographic display on Prayer for the Church Center for the United Nations. A year later, when that work was finished, approximately half of these images had been made, courtesy of the Cultural Council Foundation Artists Project—with funds provided by the New York City Department of Employment, CETA Title VI. I then became the recipient of the first annual Carl Allison Evans Award, made by Fellowship in Prayer, Inc., which enabled me to work for another year and expand the book's scope by gathering material through travels abroad.

I am indebted to Rochelle Slovin, Director of the Cultural Council Foundation Artists Project, who facilitated my sponsorship with the Church Center for the United Nations. To Dr. Melvin Hawthorne, its Chaplain, who trusted me to shape this concept as I saw fit. Above all, to Paul Griffith, Joy Reynolds, and Fellowship in Prayer's Trustees, who provided the funds and support necessary to make the vision behind this work a reality.

To my editor Toinette Lippe, for her loyalty, enthusiasm, and guidance. To my mother, Leonie, for her example of humility. To my wife, Deborah, for her encouragement, and for bearing the burden of my absences and obsessive attention to the work in hand. To my daughter, Rebecca, born six months after the start of this project, for giving me a clearer glimpse of love.

I am also grateful to the following people for opening their doors to me:

Sr. Eugene Pia and the Sister Disciples of the Divine Master, Staten Island, N.Y.; Fr. Chappell and Sr. Beth Hassel of Mount Augustine Apostolic Center, Staten Island, N.Y.; Swami Abhayananda, Swami Satchidananda and his devotees at the Integral Yoga Institute, N.Y.C.; Elizabeth Rechtschaffer, Pir Vilayat Khan and his devotees at The Abode of the Message, New Lebanon, N.Y.; Jim and Kathleen Webber, and Sharry Silvi of the Focolare Movement, N.Y.C.; Laxmi Nrshma, Devadeva, Tosan Krsna and the devotees of A. C. Bhaktivedanta Swami Prabhupada, International Society for Krsna Consciousness, in N.Y.C., and at the Gita-Nagari Farm, Port Royal, Pennsylvania; Sr. Frances Picone of the Sisters of Mercy, Brooklyn, N.Y.; Richard Robinson and the staff of the Insight Meditation Society, Barre, Mass.; Nandini Weitzman, Swami Muktananda and his devotees at Siddha Yoga Dham, N.Y.C.; Rupa and the staff of the Satgit Rajneesh Meditation Center, N.Y.C.; Eido Roshi at the New York Zendo Center; Nandini and Dr. Ramamurti Mishra of the Ananda Ashram, Monroe, N.Y.; Khair-un-nisa, Sophia, Zarifah, and Iman at the Sufi Order, N.Y.C.; Lama Norlha and his devotees at Kagyu Dsamling Kunchae, N.Y.C.; Benjamin and Menucha Levine, Brooklyn, N.Y.; Reverend Oketcho of East Harlem Interfaith, N.Y.C.; Rev. James Morton of the Cathedral of St. John the Divine, N.Y.C.; Arthur Eaton and Carla De Sola of the Omega Liturgical Dance Company, N.Y.C.; Fr. Michael Perry of the Pratt Institute, Brooklyn, N.Y.; Mother Mary Terez and the Sisters of the Dominican Nuns of Perpetual Adoration, Corpus Christi Monastery, Bronx, N.Y.; the Brothers and Sisters of Little Brothers and Little Sisters of the Gospel, N.Y.C.; Sr. Bernadette and her staff at the Dwelling Place, N.Y.C.; Dr. Natalie Maxwell and Geshe Lozang Tseten of the Lamaist Buddhist Monastery of America, Washington, N.J.; Charles Levitt of the Buddhist Church of New York, N.Y.C.; Lori Belilove of the Downtown American Dance Company, N.Y.C.; Pastor Charles Sadaphal and his congregation at the Deeper Life Christian Fellowship, Richmond Hill, N.Y.; Mr. James Shaffer of Calvary/St. George's Church, N.Y.C.; Br. Hammond and the Brothers of Weston Priory, Weston, Vermont; Janet Casper of Spiritual Frontiers Fellowship, N.Y.C.; Lama Tenzin Choney and Bardo Tulku Rinpoche of Karma Triyana Dharmachakra, Woodstock, N.Y.; Fr. Gerald Ruane of the Sacred Heart of Jesus Institute of Healing, Caldwell, N.J.; John Driscoll, Jr., M.D., and his wife, Yvonne Driscoll, M.D., and their staff at Babies Hospital, Columbia-Presbyterian Medical Center, N.Y.C.; Ibrahim Chowdry of the Islamic Council of America, N.Y.C.; Donald Lepore of the New Jersey Institute of Parapsychology, Inc., Jersey City, N.J.; Mrs. Christine Klein, Mother Ruth, and the teachers of St. Hilda's and St. Hugh's School, N.Y.C.; Monsignor Bourke, Veronica Cook, and the teachers of Corpus Christi School, N.Y.C.; Fr. O'Connor and Sr. Miriam of the Church of the Holy Name, N.Y.C.; Sr. Priscilla and the Sisters of the Missionaries of Charity, Bronx, N.Y.; Cathy and Edward Greenstein, N.Y.C.; Debby Hirshman-Green of Camp Ramah, Palmer, Mass.; Sr. Mary David and the Sisters of St. Rose's Home, N.Y.C.

A NOTE ON THE PHOTOGRAPHER

Abraham Menashe was born in Cairo, Egypt, in 1951. At age ten he emigrated with his family to the United States. He is a self-taught freelance photographer, now living in New York City with his wife, Deborah, and his daughter, Rebecca.

His photographs are in the collections of the Museum of the City of New York, the Jewish Museum, and the Metropolitan Museum of Art, New York.

In 1980 he published *Inner Grace* (Knopf), a photographic narrative on America's multihandicapped population, internationally acclaimed for its compassion and respect. The photographs, originally exhibited at the Witkin Gallery, New York City, were featured in Time-Life Books' *Photography Year/1981 Edition*, and received the One to One Media Award for publishing.

The Face of Prayer, for which he received the first Carl Allison Evans Award, is the second in a series of books which mark the author's commitment to images that affirm life, provide refuge, and offer healing.

A NOTE ON THE BOOK

The photographs were made with a Nikon FE camera equipped with a 35- or 24-mm lens. All are candid, uncropped, and made in available light. Some of these photographs form a permanent mural at the Church Center for the United Nations, 777 U.N. Plaza, New York, N.Y. The book is published in conjunction with an exhibit at the International Center of Photography, 1130 Fifth Avenue, New York, N.Y.

Fellowship in Prayer, Inc., has underwritten a major portion of this project. Since 1949 its purpose has been to promote the practice of prayer in all religious faiths that there may arise a deeper spirit of fellowship among men. It publishes a monthly magazine and is located at 20 Nassau Street, Suite 250 East, Princeton, N.J. 08540.

The text of this book was set in a film version of Bembo, the well-known monotype face. The original cutting of Bembo was made by Francesco Griffo of Bologna only a few years after Columbus discovered America. Sturdy, well-balanced, and finely proportioned, Bembo is a face of rare beauty. It is, at the same time, extremely legible in all of its sizes.

Composed by Haber Typographers Inc., New York City.
Printed in Stonetone by Rapaport Printing Corp., New York City,
on Warren's Lustro Offset Enamel Dull White, 100 lb.
Bound by The American Book-Stratford Press Company,
Saddle Brook, New Jersey.

Designed by Judith Henry.